Python Programming Tips and Tricks:

The Ultimate Cheat Sheet for Python Programming.

20+ Tips and Tricks to Make Your Life Easier and More Efficient

Table of Contents

Introduction

Congratulations on downloading *Python Programming Tips and Tricks* and thank you for doing so.

The following chapters will discuss various tips and tricks that you are going to be able to put to use when you are programming with Python.

Using Python is not easy in the first place, but with the right tips and tricks, you are going to have the skill to write out Python code that is shorter and cleaner. These tips and tricks are only going to work if you understand the basics of Python, but hopefully, they are able to help you understand everything that there is to know about Python so you can use it in a more efficient way.

Some of the code that you see in this book may appear to be complicated, and you may end up turning your head wondering how that makes it more efficient. Do not fret; it is the purpose of this book to assist you in writing out cleaner code so that you are not always turning your head wondering where you could have gone wrong. The only time that you are going to see complicated code that is not going to be broken down into an easier block of code is going to be when there is no other option for you to use.

There are plenty of books on this subject on the market, thanks again for choosing this one! Every effort was made to ensure it is full of as much useful information as possible; please enjoy!

Chapter one:
Objects and Their Truthfulness

You may have experience writing with another programming language such as JavaScript. While that is wonderful, it is not going to assist you when it comes to working with Python really.

Python is a programming language that is going to differ from most other programming languages that you have operated previously if you have not already noticed. One way that it is different from programming languages such as Javascript is that if a data type in Python is empty, it is going to be returned as false, and if it is not empty, it will be returned as true.

Python is going to check to see if the data type is empty or not, so you are not going to have to check before you place it into your program. For example, if your tuple has a length of zero or it is equal to having inserted an empty tuple, you will have tripped Python's checker to go in and check the truthfulness of the object that you have entered.

With that being said, any number that you place into Python is going to give you a truthfulness of true, but, if you enter zero, you are automatically going to get a false.

In the examples that you are going to see below, a_string is going to be your string because it is one of the types in Python that is going to be checked for truthfulness. You can use strings, tuples, lists, or dicts when you want Python to check for the integrity of the objects that are in them.

Example one:

A_string = project

#this is a true example because the string is not empty

Example two:

A_string = ‘ ‘

#this one is false due to the fact that nothing has been entered into the string actually making it an empty string.

Example three:

If len(a_string) > zero:

Print ‘a_string is not actually empty’

#due to the fact that Python considers zero to be an empty type, then you are going to get a false evaluation of your type when Python checks for the truthfulness of its objects. This is going to occur even though you do not think that it should since zero is a number, but that is not going to matter to Python because it is not how the program was written.

Chapter two:

Python Lambda Functions

There are going to be moments in your code that you need to take a function and make it pass as an argument. Or, you may realize that you are required to do an operation that is short but complex several times in a row, and you do not want to type it out as many times as you need it to be repeated.

One option you have is to define your function the normal way, or you can go with the second option which is to create a lambda function that is going to take the expression and return the proper result for how many times you need it to be repeated. No matter which plan you choos, you are going to be defining your function in the exact same way.

Example

Def subtract (c, z): result c – z

Add 3 = lambda c, z: c-z, c-z, c-z

One of the great things that you are going to discover about using the lambda function is that you are going to be using it as an expression and that means that you are going to have the knowledge to place it on a different statement.

With this example, you are going to see the map function calling on functions for every element that is located in the list which is then going to give you a list of results.
Example:

square = map (lambda c: c*c, [6, 7, 8, 2, 1])

Your result is going to be: [36, 49, 64, 4, 1]

If you did not have the lambda function, then you would be forced to define each of your functions separately. With lambda, you will save lines of code as well as variable names for the function that you are using.

The syntax for lambda functions is: lambda variable(s) : expression

Your expression is going to be a Python expression. The scope is always going to include the local scope as well as the variables. The expression is going to be what your function returns.

The variables will be the list that is separated by commas for your variables that the function is going to receive. You are not going to be able to use any keywords or parentheses. If you use parentheses, then your lambda function is not going to work properly.

Chapter three:

Using the Map and Filter Functions on Your List at the Same Time

Everyone has their own opinion when it comes to lists in Python. With the list comprehension, you are going to have the ability to use map and filter functions. Some people who use Python believe that these functions are a waste of time. But, you are going to need to make the decision for yourself on if it is worth using or not based on what you are trying to do with Python.

While you have the option of using map and filter separately, you can also use them together as well.

Let's say that you need to see the square root of every number that is under six.

Example

Num = [1, 3, 5, 7, 9]

Squares = [ ]

For num in num:

If num < 6

Squares. Append (num * num)

result: [1, 9, 25]

While you have successfully gotten the answer that you want, your code is starting to get longer, and that is not something that you are wanting to happen, you want your code to be as few lines as you can possibly make it that way if an error code occurs, you are going to have the ability to go through the code quickly in order to figure out where the error might have occurred. This is where the map and filter functions are going to come into play.

Example:

```
Num = [ 1, 3, 5, 7, 9]

Squares = map(lambda a: a*a, filter (lambda a: a < 6, num))

# result [ 1, 9, 25]
```

While the code is smaller, it is not easy to read, and that is not what you want out of the code that you are working with. If you cannot read your code, then what is the point of even using it?

Here, let's now explore what the list comprehension function would make the code look like.

Example:

```
Num = [ 1, 3, 5, 7, 9]

Squares = [ num * num for num in num if num < 6 ]

# result [ 1, 9, 25]
```

Same results and the code is much easier to read. While using the map and filter functions, you are going to get a shorter block of code; it is wiser to use a longer code block so that your script is readable.

As I stated before, you will find those who will use the map and filter functions and others that would rather change their code so that they do not have to use these functions. The choice is going to be yours, but as you can see from the examples listed above, the map and filter function is going to get complicated depending on your code.

The ultimate goal is to make your code as clean as possible, and if using these functions makes it possible, then go for it!

Chapter four:

List Comprehension Generator Expressions

List comprehension is great to use, but there is a downside to using it. Not everything is fool proof, and the biggest disadvantage to using list comprehension is that your whole list is going to have to be placed in the memory at the same time. This is not going to be a problem when your list is small and only contains a few objects. However, when your list is rather large, you are only going to be wasting your time.

Using generated expressions is something that came out with Python 2.4 and has changed the number of people who use list comprehension around. When you are using generator expressions, they are not going to load your entire list into the memory bank at once; instead, it is going to create an object that makes it to where only one element that is on the list is loaded at a time.

Should you need to use your entire list for whatever reason, using a generated expression is not really the way to go. However, if you are just trying to pass your expression off for something such as a "for" loop, then the generator function is going to work perfectly.

The syntax for a generator expression is going to be the same syntax that you use when using list comprehensions; the only difference is going to be that your parentheses are going to be on the outside of the brackets.

Example

Num = (2, 4, 6, 8)

Squares_under_30 = (num * num for num in num if num * num < 30)

any square that is under 30 will now generate an object which is going to cause each value that is successive to be called on.

For square in squares_ under_ 30:

Print square,

result: '2, 16'

While the code is not shorter like we would like it to be, it is going to be more efficient than using the list comprehension function because it is going to load your list into the memory bank one element at a time, therefore, making it to where you do not have to agonize about loading it all in at once.

In the event that you want to use this function for a list that contains more elements in it, you do have the option of using the list comprehension technique, but you should only use this if you are wanting to use your entire list at once.

However, you can use whichever method seems right for you in what you are trying to accomplish. It is recommended that you try and use the generator expressions unless you have some reason not to, but in the end, you are not going to see any real difference in the list comprehension and generator expressions unless the list that you are working with is a large list.

Keep in mind, however, that a generator expression is only going to require a single set of parentheses. Therefore, if you are calling on a function with a generator expression, you are only going to be necessary to insert a single set of parentheses.

Chapter five:

Checking Conditions for Elements in a List

There are going to be conditions that have to be met by the items that are on your list, and there will be times that you are going to want to ensure that these elements are meeting those conditions.

Should you be using Python 2.5, then your code will look similar to this:

Example:

Num = [5, 10, 15, 20, 25, 30]

If [num for num in num if num < 5]:

Print 'two elements that are over five.'

result: there are at least two items that are over five

Should there not be any elements in your list that satisfy your condition, then by default, Python is going to create an empty list and evaluate it as false. But, non-empty lists will be set up and evaluated as true if the condition is met. You do not have to assess every item that is on your list. Instead, you can quit as soon as you find one element that causes your condition to be true.

Python 2.5 has a built-in function known as any, and this function is going to do the same thing that you saw above, only your code is going to be shorter and easier to understand. With the any function, it is programmed to bail and give you a true answer after it locates the first element that satisfies your condition. This function can also be used with a generator expression so that you do not have to evaluate every element on your list and you get your true or false answer back.

Example

Num = [5, 10, 15, 20, 25, 30]

If any (num < 5 for num in num):

Output: success!

If you absolutely want to, you do have the option of checking for every element that meets your condition, if you are not using Python 2.5, then your code is going to look something like this.

Example

Num [5, 10, 15, 20, 25, 30]

If len (num) == len([num for num in num if num < 5]):

Output: success!

It is in this example that the list comprehension technique is used to filter and see if there are still as many elements that meet the condition as there were before. It is also checking to see if all of the elements are meeting the condition. Sadly, this is not an efficient way to complete this technique due to the fact that there is truly no need to check every element that is on your list to see if it satisfies the condition that you have put into place. But, if you are not using Python 2.5, this could end up being the only option that you have of checking the elements for your condition.

As you move back to Python 2.5, there is another function that you can use known as the all function. Just like the any function, this function was made to bail once it finds a single element that does not meet the condition, therefore making it to where you are given a false evaluation.

Example

```
Num = [ 5, 10, 15, 20, 25, 30]

If all (num < 5 for num in num):

Output: success!
```

Chapter six:

Converting Between a Dict and a List in Python

It is not too complicated to take a dictionary and convert it into a list. When you do this, you are going to get a list with all of the keys which will then enable you to cast that dict into a list. But, it is going to be easier and produce a cleaner code for you to use the .keys() on your dictionary so that you get the list of all of the keys in that dictionary. You can also use the .iterkeys() in order to create an iterator. This is done in the same manner that you are going to call on .values() or .itervalues so that you get a list of the values in your dictionary. It is important to remember that your dict is going to be unordered which will make it seem like the values are not in any order that is meaningful.

In an effort to save both the keys and the values of the dict, you are going to need to take that dict and turn it into a list or iterator that contains two items such as a tuple through the use of the .items() or .iteritems() function.

Example:

Dictionary = {'b' : 4 'c' : 6 'd': 8}

Dict_into_list = dict.items()

your dict_into_list will now look like this [('b': 4) ('c': 6'), ('d': 8)]

Now that you have converted your dict into a list, how do you turn it around and take your list so that it can be converted into a dict? You are going to be taking your two element list or tuple and changing it into a dict.

Example:

Dict = [('b', 4] ['c', 6], ['d', 8]

Dict _into_ list = dict.items()

your dictionary is now going to look like this: { 'b': 4, 'c' : 6, "d' : 8}

While you may be asking yourself why would you ever want to convert a dict into a list or a list into a dict, let's look at the next tip to understand how helpful knowing how to convert them really is.

Chapter seven:
Python Dictionary Comprehensions

As of this moment, Python does not have any comprehensions built in for dictionaries. So, if you are wanting a dictionary comprehension, you are going to have to write out your own code which is going to produce a piece of code that will give you the results of something that is readable and going to be reasonably similar to a list comprehension.

In order to do this, you are going to use the .iteritems() function which will convert your dict into a list as you learned in the previous chapter. From there you are going to take your list and put it through your generator expression or your list comprehension method before you turn it back into a dict.

Example:

Books = {nonfiction: WorldWarII, fiction: ‘BalladofPiney, music: LifeofBobMarley}

Books_at_library = dict([title, genre of book] for title, genere in of book books.iteritems())

Books_at_library result: {WorldWarII: true, BalladofPiney : true, LifeofBobbyMarley: false}

You have no done “dictionary comprehension!” It is not required that you start and end with a dict if you do not want to. You can always do a list or a tuple if that is what you are wanting to use instead.

The code may seem like it is less readable and straightforward than list comprehension, but it is still going to be better than working with a loop that may never end.

Chapter eight:

And/Or in Python

As you already know, using 'and' and 'or' is complicated and it is easy for you to get the two confused. When you use the and keyword, you are going to be placing two expressions together. You are not only going to get just a true statement. The 'and' statement is going to return the first value that is found to be false or the last value in the event that they are all true. So, essentially, the first value will be returned for false or the last value for true.

Due to this happening you can expect a boolean when you get the true statement which is typically done when you have used an 'if' statement. When a false evaluation is returned, then it is going to be a false boolean.

With 'or' the two expressions are going to be similar. You are going to get a result of the first value being returned if it is true or the last value is returned if they are all false. When you get a false return, you will get a false boolean. When you get that single true return, then you are going to get a true boolean.

Do not count on this to work whenever you are trying to test the truthfulness of the elements that you are working with. But, 'and' and 'or' can be used in other places in Python. One of those things would be something similar to the ternary conditional assignment operator. When you do this, you are going to be testing the elements to determine if they are true or false.

Example

Test = True

test = false

Output = test and ‘the test is true, ' or ‘the test is false.'

your result will now be printed as ‘test is true' or ‘test is false.'

In order to understand this more, you are going to look at the result that you get from your test. If you get a true, then your statement will end up skipping over it and going to the proper half where you are told that the test is true or false. However, as Python continues to execute the code from left to right, the statement will only return the first value when it is found to be true.

But in the event that your test is false, the statement will return to the test and continue its evaluation until you get the result of the test is false. Being that the test is false, the statement will be skipped over so that you get your result.

Note: you have to be careful when you are using the if_true value because it will never be returned as false. Should it be returned as false, the ‘or’ statement is going to work to skip over it and return the proper if_false value, despite what the test value really is.

‘And,' and ‘or' can be used interchangeably, so you should try both out and determine which one you prefer for the results that you are going to get. You also have the option of nesting 'and' and 'or' by adding in additional 'and's' and 'or's,' but you should only do this once you are sure that you understand how an 'and' and 'or' statement is going to work.

While this is going to seem complicated, practice it, and hopefully, you are going to be able to get the hang of it after a few times. Do not be surprised if you get some obscure results because you probably will while you are still learning how to work 'and' 'or' statements at first.

Chapter nine:

Forcing the Default Arguments to be Evaluated Every Time in a Function

Having a function that is less cluttered is going to cost you some of the readable code, but it gives you the option of forcing every default argument to be re-evaluated before the function is called. Your decorator is going to take the original value from your default argument and store it so that it can later be applied to a wrap function as well as to reset the default arguments before your call is completed.

Example:

```
From copy bring in deep copy

Def restartdefaults(a):

Defaults = a. Func_default

Def resetter (*parameter **kwds):

a.func_default = deepcopy (default)

return a (*parameter, **kwds)

restart _title_ a. _title_

return restart
```

At this point in time, the decorator is going to be applied to your function so that you get the outcomes that you are wanting.

Example

@resetdefaul # this is going to be where the decorator is applied

Def func (element, new = []):

New. Append (element)

Print new

Fun (3)

function 3 will be printed

Func (5)

function 5 will be printed as it should be.

Chapter ten:

Packages in Python – Installing the Proper Virtual Environment

Python offers a large assortment of programming ecosystems that you are going to find useful when you are writing out your code. There is a system by the name of PIP that you are going to be able to use that is not only easy to use, but it is going to be powerful when it comes to managing packages. PIP is written in order to replace the easy_install function. When you are looking at PIP from a broad standpoint, you are going to notice that there are going to be plenty of advantages to PIP that makes it superior to easy_install.

1. Any packages that are downloaded will be checked so that any partial installations can be avoided.
2. The information that is outputted is going to be processed before you see it; therefore, it makes it more useful than using eccentric messages.
3. PIP holds records to explain why actions are performed. An example of this would be as to why there is another package that is going to be required for that part of the code.
4. Whenever you are downloading packages, you can download flat modules that are going to make it to where when you debug the library code; it is going to be easier than debugging with the egg archives.
5. There is plenty of native support when it comes to the various versions of control systems that you are going to

have the option of working with. For example, you have the choice to download a package from GitHub that is going to work with Python but only if you are setting it up correctly.

6. Whenever a package has to be installed, you are going to have to manually uninstall the package which is going to avoid you from uninstalling any packages that you do not want to get rid of.
7. There is a set of requirements that are defined quite clearly when it comes to replicating sets of packages across a variety of environments.

The virtualenv tool is going to be used when you are sandboxing a Python environment. Rather than modifying the environment that is created on a global level, you are going to have the tools necessary to set up an environment that is independent and is going to look similar to all the other sandboxes, but it is going to work on its own. The biggest advantage to this is that you are not going to have to worry about any errors when you are using a different version of Python in order to test your code and the dependencies of the package. This makes it to where you do not have to switch between virtual machines.
In order to install PIP and set it up so that it works, you are going to follow this code.

#easy_install is the default package manager in CPython

% easy_install pip

#install virtualenv using pip

% pip install virtualenv

%virtualenv Python-workspace #create a virtual environment under the folder 'Python-workspace.'

In the event that you run into the error message where your Python environment does not allow you to download packages because it does not have a package manager, you are going to need to download one and run it so that you can do what you need to do to accomplish your coding goals.

At the point in time that you have set up your new virtual environment in the Python workspace folder, you have to activate it that way that the shell causes it to become the current Python environment that you are working with which is going to make transitioning into your new virtual environment easier.

Example

% dc workspace for Python

% source ./ nib/ turn on #this is going to turn the virtual environment on in the folder that you have created for it.

%Python # place your interpreter shell in here by executing your current virtual environment under the same folder that you have placed your environment in and activated it under.

Whenever you take a look at the content that is in your workspace folder you are going to see that there are several programs for you to choose from so that you can run them. One of them is going to be easy_install, and you are not going to want to use this. But, this is going to be the default program, so you are going to need to make sure that you are opening pip instead so that you are running your virtual environment in the superior package program.

Chapter eleven:

Python Decorators

We talked about decorators earlier in this book, but let's look at them a little more. A function decorator is going to be simple to use, but only if you know what is going on with the decorator and the function. Even if you do understand, the syntax may appear to be different because it is not going to be as clear as the syntax that you typically find in Python.

Decorators are going to take a function and wrap it inside of another function. Your main function is going to be called on, and the return value from that primary function is going to be passed over to the decorator. From there, the decorator is going to return the function that will then replace the wrapped function where Python is concerned.

Syntax:

Def decorator1 (func):

Return lambda: func() + 1

Def decorator2 (func):

Def print_ func ():

Print func ()

Return print _func

@decorator 2

@decorator 1

Def function () :
Return 41

Function()

#prints 42

In the following example, you are going to see that the function is going to be passed on to decorator 1 which is then going to return a function that will be called function and it will add 1. After that is done, the function is going to be passed over to the other decorator so that another function is returned that calls the function returned by the first decorator so that the result is printed. Lastly, the function will be the function that you are actually working with.

Example:

Def decorator a (function) :

Return lambda function () + one

Def decorator z (function) :

Def supply_function ():

Supply function

```
Output supply_function
Def func () :
Return 55

Func = decoratorz (decoratora (func))

Func ()

#result 55
```

Usually, a decorator will be used in an effort to add extra abilities to your function. With this being said, decorators are not used often, but it is nice to know what they are and how they work.

Chapter twelve:

Modifying Class Once Your Type has been Created

With Python, you have the option of adding, removing, or modifying the class property even after you have created it and it has been instantiated. All you are going to have to do is get into the properties of the class by using the class.attribute method. By using this method you are going to be able to make the changes, you need to make, and the class is going to have to respect the changes no matter when it was created.

Example:

Class class:

Def method (class):

Output "look I created a method."

Instance = class ()

Instance.method()

Result: "look I created a method."

Def another_method (class):

Result: "this one wins."

Class.method = another_method

Instance.method()

Output "this one wins."

You are not going to want to modify a class that already exists too much because it is going to confuse your objects that are using that class due to the fact that they are now going to have to modify to the new class which could end up causing that object to be changed as well. Whenever you modify the class too many times, the program is going to take a moment to respond to your request which is another reason that you are not going to want to do this that often. If you have an unusually long block of code that you are working with, Python may freeze up and cause you to lose everything that you have entered into the program which is going to cost you all of the time that you had spent in writing out that code.

Chapter thirteen:

Dynamic Typing in Python

When you are using most of the other programming languages that are out there, such as Java or C++ you are going to be working with a statically typed language that forces you to insert the data type of the function's returned value along with every argument that is being used with that function.

With Python, however, it is considered to be a dynamically typed programming language. When coding with Python, it is not required that you provide each data type everytime it is used in a block of code. Instead, Python uses the values that you insert into the program to keep track of any data types that are being utilized in the program.

Another way to look at dynamic typing is whenever names are tied to an object at run time, being assisted by the assignment statements. You also have the capabilities of attaching names to the objects that fall under the different types when it comes to the execution of your program. Having your program executed correctly is, of course, crucial because if it is not executed properly, then you are going to have to go back into it and change what has been messed up by your coding.

With the assistance of dynamic typing, your coding is supposed to be easier, but you are going to have to learn Python and how

you are to write out the code in the program before dynamic typing is truly going to work to your advantage.
Example

```
# a dynamic typing test

From types import *

Def check name (a):

If type (a) == internaltype:

Output "you have placed an integer into the program"

Else
Output "unable to read any data type that has been inputted."

# check for dynamic typing

Check name (543)

# outcome

# you have entered an integer

Check name ("543")

# outcome

# unable to read any data type that has been inputted.
```

Chapter fourteen:

Swapping Two Numbers In Place

Thankfully, Python gives you an instinctive that you are going to be able to perform assignments in your code along with swapping those assignments when they are in one line.

Example

A, c = 43, 23

Print (a, c)

A, c = c, a

Print (c, a)

#1 (43, 23)

#2 (23, 43)

The purpose is for your assignment to seed a new tuple. The left object is going to instantly be unpacked into a tuple that has the name of <a> and <c>.

At the point in time that your assignment has been completed, the brand new tuple will end up being unreferenced and tagged

to be deleted. The tuple where the variables were swapped will eventually be flagged as well.
The only real time that you are going to want to swap variable is whenever you have to rearrange the tuple that you are working with because you put the numbers in the wrong place. Or, you want to see how the program is going to evaluate the two numbers being switched.

You are not going to want to do this often because you are going to end up confusing yourself and the program, therefore, you should only swap the two numbers when it is absolutely necessary. Also, it is not going to work unless the variables are in the same line. If you attempt to swap two numbers that are on different lines, you are going to end up getting an error message.

Chapter fifteen:

Using a Ternary Operator with Conditional Assignments

A ternary operator is going to be the shortcut that you use when you are working with if-else statements which are also known as conditional operators.

Syntax:

[on_true] if [expression] else [on_false]

With the ternary operator, you are going to be able to make code blocks that are compact and concise which is going to be helpful should someone else be looking at your code.

In this example, you are going to see what happens if values are assigned to variables and how you are going to be able to extend the chain of operations if it is necessary.

Example

A = 5 if (b == 8) else 30

The same thing can be accomplished if you are working with class objects.

A = (class 1 if b == 3 else class 2) (arg1, arg2)

With the example you just saw, the classes are going to be two separate classes with a single class constructor that will be called on when it is needed to.

Now, this example shows how you are able to use any number of conditions in an effort to join and evaluate the smallest number that is provided.
Example

```
Def tiny ( e, f, g):

Return e if e <= f and e <= g else (f if f <= e and f <= g else g)

Print (tiny (3, 9, 3) )

Print (tiny (4, 2, 2) )

Print (tiny (1, 3,3) )

Print (tiny (5, 2, 6) )
```

Result

```
# 2 # 3 #1 # 5
```

You also have the options laid out to use ternary operators when you are working with list comprehension.

Chapter sixteen:

Metaclasses in Python and How They Work

The first thing that you need to know about metaclasses is what they are if you are not sure already. A metaclass is going to be an object or a class that will, in turn, define what class or type another class that is being used inside of your Python code. A metaclass has the option of being a class, an object, or a function that is going to be used whenever the support is needed in calling an interface. With that being said, this occurs because when a class is created for an object, the metaclass is going to be called on along with the class name and the classes attributes. Whenever there is not a metaclass that has been defined, the default type is going to be used.

Example
Python 3:
#this is where the metaclass is going to be located. It is going to point to what the metaclass object is.

Class sampleclass (metaclass = type) :

Correct

Python 2:

this is where your metaclass is going to be defined and point to the metaclass object

Class sample class (object)

metaclass = metaclass type

Correct

There are steps that the interpreter is going to follow whenever you a class in Python.

1. The name of the class has to be obtained
2. The base classes for that class need to be defined
3. The metaclass has to be created for the class. In the event that it is established it is going to be the one that is used first. If it is not defined, then it is going to go on to check the base classes that are put in for the metaclass. Should it not be able to find a metaclass inside of the base class then the object's type is going to be used.
4. The variables and the attributes for that class are going to be pulled and placed into the dictionary for use later.
5. Then, all of this information is going to be moved over to the metaclass with this syntax: metaclass (name_of_class, base_classes, attributes_dictionary) which will then return a class object.

Example

#type (the name, attributes, and base)

#what is the name of the class

#the base will be a tuple for all of the base classes where the methods and attributes are going to be inherited. It is also going to turn all the information over to the dictionary with that particular classes attributes
Class object = type ('sampleclass', (object,) , { })

Whenever the type is called on the call method is going to be used. It is this method that is going to turn the new call as well as use the init method for that call. Whenever the new method is used, a new object is going to be created, while the init method is going to be what initializes that object.

Example
Python 3

Class r

Def _init_ (self, info) :

Self. Info = info

Def getd4 (self)

Return self. Info * 4

Class themeta (type) :

Def _new_ (name of meta, class name, the bare class, the attributes) :

Print (" new call hello)

Print (name of meta, name of meta)

Print (class name, class name)

Print (the base class, the base class)

Print (the attributes, the attributes)

#the attributes [get data] = a. get d4

Return type. _new_ (name of meta, class name, the bare class, the attributes)

Def _init_ (object class, name of class, base class, attributes) :

Print (int called hello)

Print (object class, object class)

Print (name of class, name of class)

Print (class name, class name)

Print (base class, base class)

Print (attributes, attributes)

Class slk (metaclass = the meta) :

Def _init_ (self, info) :

Self. Info = info

Def printh (self)

Self. (Info = info)

Ki = slk (' nura')

Ki. Print a ()

Print (ki. Getdataa ())

The code looks complicated, and the output that you get is going to look complicated as well, however it is going to return the metaclass and everything that has to do with that metaclass which is going to make it to where you have more information about what is going on inside of the code that you are working with.

Chapter seventeen:

Detecting Which Version of Python is Being Used at Run Time

There are going to be times that the version of Python that is being used is not the version that you want your program to be executed in due to the fact that it is a version of Python that is less supported or because you think that having a different version of Python is going to cause the program to run in a different manner, and you want to see what it would do in that version. But, how are you going to be able to tell which version of Python you are using before you execute your program?

With this bit of code, you are going to be able to figure out which version of Python you are using in a block of code that is readable to you as a programmer.

Example

Import sys

figure out which version of Python is in use

If not hasattr (sys, “hexversion”) or sys. Hexversion ! = 39491183:

Print (“ you are not running this version of Python\ n”)

Print ("you need to upgrade to this version to run this program \ n")
Sys.exit (2)

print: current version of Python in a readable format

Print (“current version of Python:" sys. Version)

On the other hand, you are going to be able to use code that looks similar to this: sys. Version_info >= (version number) instead of using the hexversion bit of the code. Doing this makes it to where you can see if you are running that version of Python. It may seem like it is an easier block of code rather than the block of code that is shown in the example.

Here is what your code would look like if you were using the 2.5 version of Python.

Example

Python 2. 5. 2 (default, Jan 4, 2009, 18: 34: 12)

[GCC 4.9.1] on the Linux system

I apologize, you are not running on that version of Python

Please upgrade to the proper version of Python before trying again.

Chapter eighteen:

Four Ways to Reverse Strings and Lists

You are going to have four different ways that you can reverse the order of your strings or lists depending on what your end goal is. You are going to do this whenever it comes to fixing a mistake that you may have made, or to get a different result than what you got in the first place.

Method one: Reversing the list within itself.

With this method, you are going to be taking the list itself and changing it with a simple line of code.

Example

Sample line = [4, 2, 5]

Sample line. Reverse ()

Print (sample line)

-> [5, 3, 4]

Fairly straightforward right? All you are doing is studying the list that you have created in Python and flipping it around by reading it from the end of the line to the beginning.

Method two: Iterating within a loop

When you are iterating inside of a loop, you are still going to be reversing your list, but instead, you are going to be doing it inside of a loop which is going to cause your list to be printed out one element at a time.

Example

For object in reverse ([5, 6, 2]): print (objects)

1 -> 2

2 -> 6

3 -> 5

Method three: reverse a string inside of a line

Whenever you modify a string inside of a line, you are going to get the same result that you have been getting with the other examples that you have seen in this chapter. However, if you do not have any objects inside of that string, then you are going to be getting a different result than what you may be expecting.

Example

"Sample line" [: : -1]

Enil elpmaS

A little different correct? Well, that is alright because either way, you are getting the reversed order of your string in the line that it is occupying.

Method four: Reversing a string by using the slicing method

You have used slicing to slice the indexes for strings, lists, and tuples. But, you can also use that same method to reverse the order of a string. It is going to work the same way that you would slice an index, and you are still going to get the reverse order of the string that you have created. The code is gong to look similar to the code that you just used in method three.

[3, 1, 5] [: : -1]

Result: 5, 1, 3

So, no matter which way you use it, you are going to be getting the reverse order of your lines and strings when you use the reverse code. It is going to depend on what you are trying to accomplish in order to determine which method is going to be right for you.

You may want to practice each of these methods so that you are able to get familiar with them and understand how they work.

Chapter nineteen:

Arrays and Lists – What is the Difference?

You are able to use both arrays and lists in Python so that you can store data that you are going to use at a later time. However, they are not going to serve the same purpose while it looks like they may. Both an array and a list can contain strings, real numbers, really any data type that you are able to use inside of Python. They can also both be indexed as well as iterated. But, that is going to be where the similarities between these two data types end.

One of the biggest differences that you are going to see between arrays and lists is that the functions that you can perform with one, you are not going to be able to do with the other.

Example:

You want to take an array that you have created and divide it by 2 so that every number that is located in your array is divided by 2 and then you are going to have your result displayed on the screen should you request it. If you attempt to divide your list by the same number, you are going to receive an error message due to the fact that Python is not going to be able to complete this calculation.

A = array ([2, 4, 6, 8, 10])

A / 2.0

Print (a)

Output: 1, 2, 3, 4, 5

Seems simple enough, but what occurs when you attempt to do the same thing to a list?

A = [2, 4, 5, 6, 8, 10]

A / 2.0

Print (a)

Everything looks exactly like the first example that you saw; however, you are not going to get a valid output due to the fact that you are going to get an error.

The array is going to take an extra step due to the fact that they are going to have to be defined, unlike a list. This is the biggest reason as to why so many programmers would rather use a list over an array because they are going to already be defined in the programming language. Most of the time, a list is going to do what you want it to do, but, there are going to be times that you have to perform calculations that a list is not going to be capable of doing which will then fall on the array to complete. You may also want to contemplate using an array if you are going to be working with a large amount of data.

Chapter twenty:

Using _slots_ in Order to Reduce Memory Overheads

You may have noticed that when you are using Python, a lot of resources are consumed even with one program and one of the fastest things to be consumed is memory. However, with this trick and the use of the _slots_ class variable, you are going to have the ability to reduce the overhead for memory. This is not going to reduce it completely, but it will reduce it a significant amount so that you have more open memory to work with as you write your programs.

Example

Import sys

Class filesystem (element):

Def _init_ (class, docs, folders, devices) :

Class. Docs = docs

Class. Folders = folders

Class. Devices = devices

Print (sys. Get size of (filesystem))
Class file system (element) :

```
_slots _ = [ docs, folders, devices ]

Def _int_ (class, docs, folders, devices) :

Class. Docs = docs
Class. Folders = folders

Class. Devices = devices

Print (sys. Getsizeof ( filesystem2 ) )

#output

# 1 -> 4294

# 2 -> 949
```

It is easy to see from the output just how much memory that you are saving when you use the _slots_ method. However, you only need to be using this method when it comes to the overhead for a class that is larger than it has to be. Make sure that you are only doing it after you have profiled the application. If you do it any other time, then the code is going to be complicated and unable to be changed which will be no real benefit to you.

Due to the fact that you are only going to want to do this with the larger classes, you are going to want to create a few examples in which you would need to use this technique so that you can get some practice with it. It is rare that you will be using it and if you do not understand how it works, then how are you going to know when to use it and how it is supposed to look in your code?

Chapter twenty-one:

Forming Unified Lists Without the Aid of a Loop

Example

Import itertools

Sample = [[-2, -4] , [40, 59]. [39, 29]]

Output (list (itertools. Chain. From_iterable (sample)))

Result -> -2, -4, 40, 59, 39, 29

After you have inserted your list into Python by using lists or tuples that have been nested you are going to use a different set of code. Keep in mind though that there are going to be limitations on what this code is going to actually be able to do when you are using a ‘for’ loop.

Example

Def unifysample (s_ input, s_target):

For it in s_input

Ifisinstance (it, sample) :

Unifysample (it, s_target)

Elif isinstance (it, list) :
Unifysample (tuple (it), s_ target)

Else:

S_target. Append (it)

Result s_target

Sample = [[-3, -2], [2, 4, 5, [8, (9, [3, 4])]], (39, 10), [49, 92]]

Print (unifysample (test, [ ]))

Result => -3, -2, 2, 4, 5, 8, 9, 3, 4, 39, 10, 49, 92

In using this technique, you are going to be able to use a method that is simpler in unifying the list, and that is nested with a list or tuple. All you are going to need to do is use the < more_itertool> module that Python has to offer.

While using this technique, you are going to be able to bypass having to create a loop which is going to be nice because you never know when an infinite loop is going to be created therefore causing you to have to terminate the program.

Instead, all you are going to need to do is insert this little snippet of code that is going to allow you to use this method without the loop.

Syntax

<pip install more_itertools>

Example

Import more_itertools

Sample = [[-3, -2], [2, 4, 5, [8, (9, [3, 4])]], (39, 10), [49, 92]]

Print (list (more_itertools. Resize (sample)))

Output => -3, -2, 2, 4, 5, 8, 9, 3, 4, 39, 10, 49, 92

You will see that between the two different methods, while you are getting the same result, you are going through more moves than necessary with the first one, therefore, making your code longer and potentially unreadable.

Chapter twenty-two:

Checking for Odd and Even Numbers with Python

Python makes it easy to calculate expressions. One thing that you may discover about Python is that it gives you the option of figuring out what the remainder is going to be whenever one number is divided by another. However, in order to do this, you are going to be required to use a modulo symbol between the two numbers so that Python calculates what the remainder is going to be whenever the first number is divided by the second one.

In the event that the second number goes into the first one evenly, you are going to get an answer of zero due to the fact that you are not going to have a remainder. But, on the other hand, if the number does not go into the first evenly, you are going to get some sort of remainder.

Example

4 % 2

10 % 4

When you look at the first example, you are going to get an answer of zero due to the fact that 2 is going to go into 4 evenly. That is the simple part. The more involved part is going to come when you look at the second part of the example.

Modulo is going to be used when you are trying to determine what the remainder is going to be once the calculation has been performed. Therefore, you are not trying to discover what the actual answer is going to be for 10 % 4.

10 % 4 is going to give you a remainder of 2 because 4 is going to go into 10 at least 2 times evenly, but it is not going entirely to give you an answer of ten, hence why your answer is two.

One thing that you are able to use modulo for is to test and see if there are any even numbers or odd numbers in your calculations. Should a number be divided by two and not have a remainder, then that is going to be considered an even number. However, if you can divide by two and still get a remainder, you are going to get what is considered to be an odd number.

Example

If (num % 2 == 0: # the number will be even. You will place this code in your program to be executed.

Else: #number is odd, the code will need to be inserted into this space.

Essentially, should a remainder be divided by 2, your answer is zero. If it is not zero, then you are working with an odd number.

The code that you saw above is going to be able to be used when you are executing numbers from various functions just as long as your question is if the number is even or odd. When the code states to put your code here, you are going to need to add some functionality to your code so that it does what you are wanting it to do.

Chapter twenty-three:

The Help () Function

Python has a module that is built into it that is going to be known as the help () function that will give you the documentation that Python has based off of a variety of attributes, methods, and objects. If you are a beginner of Python, then this is going to be a function that you are going to want to look into.

To pass this object, you are going to need to set the parameters for your help () function and get a new background that is going to work with the official documentation that Python has to offer you.

Example:

If you are wanting to get some data on tuples and what you are able to do with them in Python. You are going to enter a simple code that is going to bring up everything that you are wanting to know about tuples in Python.

Help(tup)

As stated previously, the output for your function is going to give you detailed information that is going to be informative about what it is that you are trying to gain more information about. You will get this information in the Python program in the form of help messages.

If you are a beginner to Python, this is one tip you are definitely going to want to put in your toolbox as you go through your beginning stages of learning about Python and all it has to offer.

Chapter twenty-four:

The Python Package Index Also Known As PyPi

Python Package Index is going to be a repository for software that was created specifically for Python and the language that it is written in. Therefore, should you be looking for a package or even a module to use for your code, you are going to find it with PyPi most likely. Any package that you find with PyPi is going to be able to be installed through the command line of PIP.

It is with Pypi; you are going to have the option of downloading packages or posting them in the event that you have written a package that you think is going to assist others with their coding projects that they are going to be working on with Python.

Any packages that are found in the Python Package Index are going to be open sourced, which means that if you are going to install something from PyPi, you are going to have the capabilities to modify the code so that it is able to suit what you need it to do.

In the event that you are uploading a package that you have written, then you will be required to have a user account, you will need to register your project, tell what your project is, and the package for your project before you are able to upload it to the PyPi memory bank.

If you do not follow the rules that are set into place by Python in an effort to get your package uploaded, then you are going to run into problems, and ultimately, your package is not going to be open for anyone to get to because it is not going to be in Python.

As a developer, you are going to want to check into PyPi. You are never going to know who you are going to help by uploading your own package coding. It could be the difference of someone having to use a package that gives them what they need for half of their project and using your package which could end up giving them everything that they need which in turn could be one of the greatest discovers in technology as we know it.

As a member of the Python society, you are going to want to go to the PyPi interface and check out what Python has to offer. You never know what you will find and what is going to be there that will give you that small push that you have been looking for in order to finish one of your projects.

Chapter twenty-five:

The True Difference between _str_ and _repr_ functions in Python

Python officially defines the _str_ and _repr_ functions as follows.

Object. _repr_ (self) : called by the repr () built-in function and by string conversions (reverse quotes) to complete the official string representation of an object.

Object. _str_ (self) : called by the str () build in function and by the print statement to compute the informal string representation of an object.

It is also from the official documents that have been put out by those that work on Python that we are able to gain the knowledge to know that the _str_ and _repr_ functions are going to be used when trying to represent an object.

The _repr_ function is going to be the official representation of that object while the _str_ function is going to be the informal one.

With this knowledge comes a new question, what will the default implementation of an object with these functions look like?

Example

Let's say that we are using int a and str I in the expression that we are inputting into Python and this is going to be done by using the two functions.

A = 2

Repr (a)

‘2.'

Str (a)

“2."

I = i string

Repr (i)

‘I string.'

Str (i)

“I string."

Looking at the code, you are going to notice that the output for both functions is precisely the same, however, look closer and you are going to realize that the biggest difference between the two outputs is that different quotes are being used in each of the answers for these functions. You have to realize that whenever a default implementation of _repr_ is utilized for the str object, you are going to be calling on it as an argument so that it is evaluated and then having a value returned in order to be a valid str object.

Example

Repr (a)

" ' the string.' "

a8 = eval (repr (a))

a = = a 8

correct

In the event that the value that is returned for a _str_ is not even, then a statement that is valid will be executed by the eval piece of your code.

Example

Str (r)

' " the string " '

Eval (str (r))

Follow (the last call that was made) :

File <nidts> line 4 in <module>

File <string>, line 4

The string

Error syntax: there was an unexpected error that occurred while parsing.

With that being said, a representation that is considered to be formal for an object is going to be called on by the eval() function, and it should return the same object if the block of code is going to allow it to happen. If it is not allowed, which would be whenever the members of an object refer to itself, then an infinite circular reference is going to be started which is then going to cause _repr_ to be unambiguous which will then hold as much information as it is allowed to hold.

Example

```
Class classx (element) :

Def _init_ (class, e = none) :

Class. E = e

Def _repr_ (class) :

Return '% (%r)' % (class . _class_. Class. E_

Class classf (element) :

Def _init_ (class, q = none) :

Class. F = f

Def _repr_ (class) :

Return "% (%r)" % (class _class_, class. F)

Q = classf ()

x= classe (f = f)

q.x = e

repr (e)
```

runtime error: there are too many recursions used while calling upon an element in Python.

So, rather than follow the requirement that is set in place for _repr_ literally due to the fact that it is going to always result in an infinite recursion, you will change the class to something different. One way that you can do this is to locate as much information as yu can about the element that you are working with before putting it into the code. You are going to want to make sure it is equal to an eval confined _repr_.

Example

Class classe (element) :

Def _init_ (class, g = none) :

Class. G = g

Def _repr_ (class) :

Return ‘%s (g = g)’ % (class. _class_)

E = class g ()

W = class l (g = g)

e. w = l

repr (g)

<the class for the main part of a is going to be equal to class be.>

Repr (l)

<class ‘_main_. Class l ‘ > (g = g)”

Due to the fact that the _repr_ function is always going to be the most official representation for any element, you are always going to want to write it "repr (an_eleme)" so that you are capable to get the most informative information that you can about that particular object.

But, there will be times that using _str_ is going to be helpful since _repr) is going to cause your code to be too complicated and you are not going to have the option of checking to see if your element is complex. Think of it as an object that has about a dozen different attributes. This is where _str_ is going to come in handy so that you are able to get a quick rundown of the most complex elements.

Example

Say that you want to look at a date/time element that is located in the middle of a log file in order to figure out why the date/ time on an employee's records is not correct.

From date/time import date/time

Now = date/time. Current ()

Repr (current)

Date/time. Date/time (2001, 4, 3, 6, 23, 11, 480958)

Str (current)

2001-04-03 06: 23: 11. 480958)
By using the _str_ function, your code is now cleaner and easier to read than if you had gone through and used the _repr_ function. While you would have gotten the same result,

the code that you would have had to insert into Python would have been too much to handle when an error occurred.

It is sometimes a good thing to be able to look at what is inside of the object and get the general overall picture of what is going on rather than to look at all the intimate details of a complex program.

Conclusion

Thank you for making it through to the end of *Python Programming Tip sand Tricks*, let's hope it was informative and able to provide you with all of the tools you need to achieve your goals whatever it may be.

The next step is to find the tips and tricks that are going to pertain to what you are doing in your life and make them work for you! Not every tip that was listed in this book is going to work for the code that you are working with, and if it doesn't that is okay, you are going to be able to find something else that works for you.

Just remember that you need to be patient as you go about programming Python. It is not going to be easy, but you will be able to accomplish what you are wanting to achieve, even if it takes you a few tries.

Finally, if you found this book useful in any way, a review on Amazon is always appreciated!

Thank you and good luck!

www.ingramcontent.com/pod-product-compliance
Lightning Source LLC
Chambersburg PA
CBHW070855070326
40690CB00009B/1857

* 9 7 8 1 5 4 7 0 3 9 2 3 4 *